THE MOST POWERFUL PRESIDENTIAL WORDS

ASK NOT WHAT YOUR COUNTRY CAN DO FOR YOU; ASK WHAT YOU CAN DO FOR YOUR COUNTRY

BY KATIE KAWA

Gareth Stevens
PUBLISHING

Please visit our website, www.garethstevens.com. For a free color catalog of all our high-quality books, call toll free 1-800-542-2595 or fax 1-877-542-2596.

Library of Congress Cataloging-in-Publication Data

Names: Kawa, Katie, author.
Title: The most powerful presidential words / Katie Kawa.
Description: New York : Gareth Stevens Publishing, 2020. | Series: Words
  that shaped america | Includes index. |
Identifiers: LCCN 2019026842 | ISBN 9781538247969 | ISBN 9781538247976
  (library binding) | ISBN 9781538247952 (paperback) | ISBN 9781538247983
  (ebook)
Subjects: LCSH: Presidents--United States--Quotations--Juvenile works. |
  United States--Politics and government--Quotations--Juvenile works. |
  Speeches, addresses, etc., American--Juvenile works. | Political
  oratory--United States--Juvenile works.
Classification: LCC E176.8 .K39 2020 | DDC 080.973--dc23
LC record available at https://lccn.loc.gov/2019026842

First Edition

Published in 2020 by
Gareth Stevens Publishing
111 East 14th Street, Suite 349
New York, NY 10003

Designer: Sarah Liddell
Editor: Therese Shea

Photo credits: Cover, p. 1 (main) Hohum/Wikimedia Commons; cover, p. 1 (inset) DoxTxob/
Wikimedia Commons; ink smear used throughout Itsmesimon/Shutterstock.com; border used
throughout igorrita/Shutterstock.com; background used throughout Lukasz Szwaj/
Shutterstock.com; p. 5 (Oath of Office) Bettmann/Contributor/Bettmann/Getty Images;
p. 5 (State of the Union Address) Donaldson Collection/Contributor/Michael Ochs Archives/
Getty Images; p. 7 (George Washington) Alonso de Mendoza/Wikimedia Commons;
p. 7 (Farewell Address) SilkTork/Shutterstock.com; p. 8 Inefable001/Shutterstock.com;
p. 9 Wow/Wikimedia Commons; p. 10 Everett Historical/Shutterstock.com; p. 11 (Gettysburg
Address) Adam Parent/Shutterstock.com; p. 11 (Gettysburg, Pennsylvania) Jon Bilous/
Shutterstock.com; p. 13 (Inaugural Address) WFinch/Wikimedia Commons; p. 13 (fireside chat)
Hulton Archive/Stringer/Archive Photos/Getty Images; p. 15 (Winston Churchill) Fæ/
Wikimedia Commons; p. 15 (Roosevelt's message to Congress) MPI/Stringer/Archive Photos/
Getty Images; p. 17 (Inaugural Address) George Silk/Contributor/The LIFE Picture Collection/
Getty Images; p. 17 (*Friendship 7*) Photo 12/Contributor/Universal Images Group/Getty Images;
p. 19 Davepape/Wikimedia Commons; p. 21 (newspaper) Blank Archives/Contributor/Archive
Photos/Getty Images; p. 21 (Nixon) Wehwalt/Wikimedia Commons; p. 23 (Berlin Wall) picture
alliance/Contributor/picture alliance/Getty Images; p. 23 (Reagan) AFP/Stringer/AFP/
Getty Images; p. 25 The White House/Handout/Getty Images News/Getty Images; p. 27 (The
Obamas) Ralf-Finn Hestoft/Contributor/Corbis Historical/Getty Images; p. 27 (sign)
Mondadori Portfolio/Contributor/Mondadori Portfolio/Getty Images.

Printed in the United States of America

Some of the images in this book illustrate individuals who are models. The depictions do not
imply actual situations or events.

CPSIA compliance information: Batch #CW20GS: For further information contact Gareth Stevens, New York, New York at 1-800-542-2595.

CONTENTS

Words in the glossary appear in **bold** type
the first time they are used in the text.

SOLEMN OATH

When a person becomes US president, they say the same words—called the oath of office—that every president has said since the United States became its own country: "I do solemnly swear (or affirm) that I will faithfully execute the office of president of the United States, and will to the best of my ability, preserve, protect and defend the Constitution of the United States."

These 35 words are some of the most powerful in American history, but they're not the only powerful words a president

BEHIND THE WORDS

THE OATH OF OFFICE IS MENTIONED IN THE US CONSTITUTION. IT WAS FIRST SAID IN 1789 WHEN GEORGE WASHINGTON BECAME THE COUNTRY'S FIRST PRESIDENT.

speaks during their time in office. From offering advice for the future and hope for the present to dealing with other countries and even declaring war, the words spoken by US presidents have changed the world!

BIG MOMENTS

Some presidents address the American people more often than others. However, they all have to speak during certain events. For example, the US Constitution states that a president must give a State of the Union Address. This is a speech in front of Congress in which they talk about their plans for the country. Presidents are also expected to give a speech when they first take office—an inaugural address—and when they leave—a farewell address.

Every president has their own way with words, but they all start their time in office with the same oath.

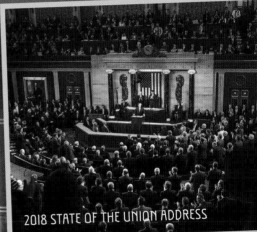

2018 STATE OF THE UNION ADDRESS

GEORGE WASHINGTON TAKING OATH OF OFFICE

WASHINGTON SAYS GOODBYE

George Washington was the first president to take the oath of office, and he was also the first president to deliver a farewell address. In this address, he said that "the shade of retirement is as necessary to me as it will be welcome." He wanted to spend his last years living among his fellow citizens, and his farewell address was his final goodbye to them as president.

Washington could have kept being president as long as he wanted. Today, a president can serve for only two terms, but that wasn't true during Washington's time. Many people wanted him to be president as long as he lived! However, he knew it was right for him—and for the United States—to step aside and let someone else lead the country.

BEHIND THE WORDS

GEORGE WASHINGTON GOT HELP WRITING HIS FAREWELL ADDRESS FROM ALEXANDER HAMILTON, THE SUBJECT OF THE MUSICAL *HAMILTON*. PARTS OF THE FAREWELL ADDRESS ARE INCLUDED IN THE SONG "ONE LAST TIME."

WASHINGTON'S FAREWELL ADDRESS WAS SHARED ACROSS THE NATION IN 1796. IT'S STILL CONSIDERED ONE OF THE MOST IMPORTANT ADDRESSES IN AMERICAN HISTORY.

GEORGE WASHINGTON

FINAL ADVICE

In his farewell address, Washington gave some final advice to his fellow Americans. He told them that they should focus more on what they have in common as Americans and less on the divisions between different parts of the country. He also warned about the dangers of getting involved in other countries' problems and of political parties that work against each other. In fact, he said that political parties are a government's "worst enemy."

THE MONROE DOCTRINE

Some presidents have become famous for the words they've said about other countries. James Monroe was one such president. On December 2, 1823, Monroe delivered an address to Congress. It became known as the Monroe **Doctrine**.

Monroe said that "the American continents . . . are henceforth [from now on] not to be considered as subjects for future colonization by any European powers." At that time, **Latin American** countries were becoming independent nations, but some Americans feared

European countries, especially Spain, would try to make them colonies again. This would threaten the United States, which was still a new country and not very powerful. By declaring this statement, Monroe helped make sure the United States was the most powerful influence in the Americas.

DEFINING THE DOCTRINE

The Monroe Doctrine did more than just order European nations to stay out of the Americas. It also said that the United States would stay out of the business of European countries, including colonies European countries already had. The meaning of the Monroe Doctrine changed over time. In 1904, President Theodore Roosevelt used it to justify acting as "an international police power" in Latin America. This expansion of the Monroe Doctrine is known as the Roosevelt **Corollary**.

JAMES MONROE

MONROE'S WORDS CHANGED US FOREIGN POLICY—THE WAY THE UNITED STATES DEALS WITH OTHER COUNTRIES.

BEHIND THE WORDS

JAMES MONROE ASKED THOMAS JEFFERSON FOR ADVICE ABOUT FOREIGN POLICY. JEFFERSON, US PRESIDENT FROM 1801 TO 1809, IS MOST FAMOUS FOR WORDS HE WROTE BEFORE BECOMING PRESIDENT—THE DECLARATION OF INDEPENDENCE.

THE GETTYSBURG ADDRESS

Abraham Lincoln was president during one of the most difficult periods in American history. After he became president in 1861, a group of Southern states, hoping to preserve the institution of slavery, broke away from the rest of the union to form the Confederate States of America. This led to the American Civil War.

One of the most important battles in the Civil War was the Battle of Gettysburg. On November 19, 1863, Lincoln visited Gettysburg, Pennsylvania, and gave a speech that became known as the Gettysburg Address. Lincoln honored the men who fought there: "The world will little note, nor long remember what we say here, but it can never forget what they did here." He was wrong, though; the world has remembered what he said for more than 150 years!

BEHIND THE WORDS

BEFORE LINCOLN'S ADDRESS, FAMOUS SPEAKER EDWARD EVERETT TALKED FOR 2 HOURS. EVERETT LATER TOLD LINCOLN, "I WISH THAT I COULD FLATTER MYSELF THAT I HAD COME AS NEAR TO THE CENTRAL IDEA OF THE OCCASION, IN TWO HOURS, AS YOU DID IN TWO MINUTES."

FOUR SCORE AND SEVEN YEARS AGO OUR FATHERS BROUGHT FORTH ON THIS CONTINENT A NEW NATION CONCEIVED IN LIBERTY AND DEDICATED TO THE PROPOSITION THAT ALL MEN ARE CREATED EQUAL.

NOW WE ARE ENGAGED IN A GREAT CIVIL WAR TESTING WHETHER THAT NATION OR ANY NATION SO CONCEIVED AND SO DEDICATED CAN LONG ENDURE · WE ARE MET ON A GREAT BATTLEFIELD OF THAT WAR · WE HAVE COME TO DEDICATE A PORTION OF THAT FIELD AS A FINAL RESTING PLACE FOR THOSE WHO HERE GAVE THEIR LIVES THAT THAT NATION MIGHT LIVE · IT IS ALTOGETHER FITTING AND PROPER THAT WE SHOULD DO THIS · BUT IN A LARGER SENSE WE CAN NOT DEDICATE—WE CAN NOT CONSECRATE—WE CAN NOT HALLOW-THIS GROUND · THE BRAVE MEN LIVING AND DEAD WHO STRUGGLED HERE HAVE CONSECRATED IT FAR ABOVE OUR POOR POWER TO ADD OR DETRACT · THE WORLD WILL LITTLE NOTE NOR LONG REMEMBER WHAT WE SAY HERE BUT IT CAN NEVER FORGET WHAT THEY DID HERE · IT IS FOR US THE LIVING RATHER TO BE DEDICATED HERE TO THE UNFINISHED WORK WHICH THEY WHO FOUGHT HERE HAVE THUS FAR SO NOBLY ADVANCED · IT IS RATHER FOR US TO BE HERE DEDICATED TO THE GREAT TASK REMAINING BEFORE US-THAT FROM THESE HONORED DEAD WE TAKE INCREASED DEVOTION TO THAT CAUSE FOR WHICH THEY GAVE THE LAST FULL MEASURE OF DEVOTION-THAT WE HERE HIGHLY RESOLVE THAT THESE DEAD SHALL NOT HAVE DIED IN VAIN-THAT THIS NATION UNDER GOD SHALL HAVE A NEW BIRTH OF FREEDOM-AND THAT GOVERNMENT OF THE PEOPLE BY THE PEOPLE FOR THE PEOPLE SHALL NOT PERISH FROM THE EARTH·

GETTYSBURG, PENNSYLVANIA

LINCOLN DELIVERED THE GETTYSBURG ADDRESS AT THE **DEDICATION** OF A CEMETERY THAT WAS CREATED WHERE THE BATTLE OF GETTYSBURG TOOK PLACE. PEOPLE CAN STILL VISIT THIS SITE TODAY.

A FAMOUS BEGINNING

THE GETTYSBURG ADDRESS HAS ONE OF THE MOST FAMOUS OPENING LINES OF ALL TIME: "FOUR SCORE AND SEVEN YEARS AGO OUR FATHERS BROUGHT FORTH ON THIS CONTINENT A NEW NATION . . ." IN ORDER TO UNDERSTAND WHAT IT MEANS, YOU NEED TO DO SOME MATH! A SCORE IS 20 YEARS, SO "FOUR SCORE AND SEVEN YEARS" IS 87 YEARS. THAT'S HOW MUCH TIME PASSED BETWEEN THE SIGNING OF THE DECLARATION OF INDEPENDENCE AND THE GETTYSBURG ADDRESS.

FDR ON
FEAR

Like Lincoln, Franklin Delano Roosevelt was president during a hard time for Americans. When he delivered his inaugural address on March 4, 1933, the United States was in the middle of the Great Depression. This was a period of economic problems that left millions of Americans without jobs. People needed hope, and Roosevelt tried to give it to them.

During his speech, Roosevelt told Americans, "So, first of all, let me **assert** my firm belief that the only thing we have to fear is fear itself." During the Great Depression, people were afraid of many things, including losing their jobs and their homes. However, Roosevelt wanted them to feel hopeful about the future instead of afraid. He used his speech to give them reasons to believe things were going to get better.

BEHIND THE WORDS

DURING HIS TIME AS PRESIDENT, ROOSEVELT COMMUNICATED DIRECTLY WITH THE AMERICAN PEOPLE OVER THE RADIO. ROOSEVELT USED CLEAR LANGUAGE AND A COMFORTING TONE DURING THESE ADDRESSES, WHICH CAME TO BE KNOWN AS FIRESIDE CHATS.

FRANKLIN D. ROOSEVELT, OFTEN CALLED FDR, HELPED AMERICANS GET THROUGH THE GREAT DEPRESSION WITH THE POWER OF HIS INSPIRING WORDS. SOMETIMES THE MOST IMPORTANT THING A PRESIDENT CAN DO IS COMFORT THE NATION WHEN TIMES ARE TOUGH.

THE NEW DEAL

THE GREAT DEPRESSION BEGAN IN 1929. BY THE TIME ROOSEVELT GAVE HIS FIRST INAUGURAL ADDRESS, ALMOST 13 MILLION AMERICANS WERE OUT OF WORK. ROOSEVELT HELPED THOSE PEOPLE BY USING HIS PRESIDENTIAL POWER TO START PROGRAMS THAT CREATED JOBS, AIDED FARMERS, AND GAVE THE GOVERNMENT CONTROL OVER CERTAIN PARTS OF THE ECONOMY. THIS SERIES OF PROGRAMS WAS CALLED THE NEW DEAL. IT GAVE THE FEDERAL GOVERNMENT MORE POWER THAN IT HAD EVER HAD BEFORE.

THE WORLD AT WAR

Franklin D. Roosevelt's words helped people deal with the Great Depression, and they also comforted Americans as the world went to war. The United States stayed out of World War II at first, but on December 7, 1941, Japan attacked the US naval base at Pearl Harbor in Hawaii. Many Americans were killed and ships destroyed.

The next day, Roosevelt asked Congress to declare war on Japan. In his address, he called the day of the attack "a date

BEHIND THE WORDS

THE AMERICAN PEOPLE BELIEVED IN FDR SO MUCH THAT THEY ELECTED HIM PRESIDENT FOUR TIMES. HE'S THE ONLY PRESIDENT TO SERVE MORE THAN TWO TERMS. THE CONSTITUTION WAS LATER CHANGED SO PRESIDENTS COULDN'T BE ELECTED MORE THAN TWO TIMES.

which will live in **infamy**." Roosevelt's address brought the United States into World War II, the deadliest war in history. By the time the war ended in 1945, it had taken the lives of more than 55 million people around the world.

POWERFUL WORDS ACROSS THE POND

ROOSEVELT WASN'T THE ONLY LEADER WHOSE WORDS HELPED HIS COUNTRY DURING WORLD WAR II. PRIME MINISTER WINSTON CHURCHILL WAS THE LEADER OF THE BRITISH GOVERNMENT DURING THIS TIME. HE GAVE SPEECHES THAT INSPIRED THE BRITISH PEOPLE TO KEEP FIGHTING. IN A SPEECH FROM 1940, HE SAID, "WE SHALL FIGHT ON THE BEACHES, WE SHALL FIGHT ON THE LANDING GROUNDS, WE SHALL FIGHT IN THE FIELDS AND IN THE STREETS, WE SHALL FIGHT IN THE HILLS; WE SHALL NEVER SURRENDER."

WINSTON CHURCHILL

ROOSEVELT MADE CHANGES TO THE FIRST DRAFT, OR VERSION, OF HIS ADDRESS. ONE IMPORTANT CHANGE WAS SAYING "A DATE WHICH WILL LIVE IN INFAMY" RATHER THAN "A DATE WHICH WILL LIVE IN WORLD HISTORY."

15

A NEW LEADER FOR A NEW GENERATION

Another president whose words inspired Americans was John F. Kennedy. He was a young president—only 43 years old when he took office—and people believed he could create lasting, positive change.

Kennedy delivered his inaugural address on January 20, 1961. In it, he said, "The torch has been passed to a new generation of Americans," who had a responsibility to make their country—and the world—a better place.

In the most famous line from his inaugural address, Kennedy advised his fellow Americans, "Ask not what your country can do for you—ask what you can do for your country." This call to citizenship helped define a new age of **activism** in the United States, especially for young Americans.

BEHIND THE WORDS

JOHN F. KENNEDY NEVER GOT THE CHANCE TO DELIVER A SECOND INAUGURAL ADDRESS. HE WAS SHOT AND KILLED IN DALLAS, TEXAS, ON NOVEMBER 22, 1963.

THE 1960s WAS A DECADE OF BIG CHANGES IN THE UNITED STATES. MANY YOUNG PEOPLE RESPONDED TO KENNEDY'S CALL TO ACTIVISM.

A SPEECH ABOUT SPACE

IN THE EARLY 1960s, THE UNITED STATES WAS FALLING BEHIND THE **SOVIET UNION** IN THE RACE TO EXPLORE SPACE. KENNEDY, HOWEVER, WANTED TO CHANGE THAT. IN A SPEECH IN 1962, HE SAID, "WE CHOOSE TO GO TO THE MOON IN THIS DECADE AND DO THE OTHER THINGS, NOT BECAUSE THEY ARE EASY, BUT BECAUSE THEY ARE HARD." KENNEDY'S BELIEF PAID OFF: IN 1969, THE UNITED STATES BECAME THE FIRST COUNTRY TO REACH THE MOON.

"WE SHALL OVERCOME"

After Kennedy's death, his vice president, Lyndon B. Johnson, became president. The civil rights movement, which had begun in the 1950s, continued to grow during Johnson's time as president. He spoke out about the need for equal rights—especially voting rights—for all Americans.

BEHIND THE WORDS

THE FAMOUS CIVIL RIGHTS LEADER MARTIN LUTHER KING JR. WATCHED JOHNSON'S ADDRESS TO CONGRESS. HE WAS ONE OF MANY AMERICANS, BLACK AND WHITE, WHO WERE SO MOVED THEY CRIED.

On March 15, 1965, Johnson addressed Congress about the importance of creating a law that protected voting rights for African Americans. He said, "Their cause must be our cause too. Because . . . really it is all of us, who must overcome the crippling legacy of **bigotry** and injustice. And we shall overcome." "We Shall Overcome" is a song African Americans often sang while marching for their civil rights. By using those words, Johnson made those fighting for equal rights believe he was fighting beside them.

SPEAKING ABOUT SELMA

Johnson's address to Congress came just over a week after state troopers attacked people marching for voting rights in Selma, Alabama. The violence left many badly hurt. The attack was shown on television news programs across the country, which made many people more aware of the civil rights movement. As Johnson said in his speech, what happened in Selma—an event often called Bloody Sunday—was "a turning point in man's unending search for freedom."

Johnson's speech led to real change. On August 6, 1965, Johnson signed the Voting Rights Act. This act banned many of the practices that kept African Americans from being allowed to vote.

JOHNSON SHAKING HANDS WITH MARTIN LUTHER KING JR.

NIXON STEPS DOWN

A president's words don't always have to be positive to be powerful. This was the case for Richard Nixon, whose presidency became known more for **scandal** than for anything else. The Watergate scandal involved a break-in at the offices of Nixon's political opponents. As Nixon's efforts to cover up this scandal became more widely known, it became clear to the president that his best option was to resign.

Nixon made his decision public on August 8, 1974. In a speech to the American people, he said, "I have never been a quitter . . . But as president, I must put the interest of America first . . . Therefore, I shall resign the presidency effective at noon tomorrow." This was the first time in US history that a president resigned.

BEHIND THE WORDS

BEFORE NIXON RESIGNED, HE CONTINUED TO DENY THAT HE'D DONE ANYTHING WRONG. HE FAMOUSLY TOLD REPORTERS, "I AM NOT A CROOK."

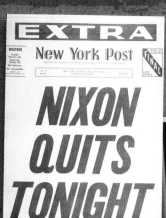

MANY PARTS OF THE WATERGATE SCANDAL, INCLUDING NIXON'S RESIGNATION ANNOUNCEMENT, WERE SHOWN ON TELEVISION. THAT GAVE MILLIONS OF AMERICANS A CLOSE-UP VIEW AS THIS CHAPTER IN US HISTORY UNFOLDED.

WHAT'S WATERGATE?

THE WATERGATE SCANDAL GOT ITS NAME FROM THE WATERGATE BUILDING COMPLEX OF OFFICES, HOTEL ROOMS, AND APARTMENTS. SOME WATERGATE OFFICES BELONGED TO THE DEMOCRATIC NATIONAL COMMITTEE, THE GOVERNING BODY FOR THE DEMOCRATIC PARTY. ON JUNE 17, 1972, FIVE MEN WERE ARRESTED FOR BREAKING IN TO THOSE OFFICES. THE BREAK-IN WAS SOON CONNECTED TO THE REELECTION CAMPAIGN FOR NIXON, A REPUBLICAN. EVENTUALLY, INVESTIGATIONS MADE CLEAR THAT NIXON HIMSELF WAS TRYING TO COVER UP FACTS ABOUT ILLEGAL ACTIVITIES.

REAGAN AT THE
BERLIN WALL

For many years, the United States and the Soviet Union and these countries' allies were involved in what was known as the Cold War. Rather than all-out military warfare, this was a tense period between countries that supported communism, such as the Soviet Union, and those that didn't, such as the United States.

One of the most famous symbols of the Cold War was the Berlin Wall in Germany. On June 12, 1987, President Ronald Reagan spoke in front of the part of the wall called Brandenburg Gate. He addressed Mikhail Gorbachev, who was the leader of the Soviet Union at the time: "Mr. Gorbachev, tear down this wall!" The Berlin Wall was torn down 2 years later as the Cold War was coming to an end.

BEHIND THE WORDS

RONALD REAGAN WAS SUCH A GOOD SPEAKER THAT HE WAS CALLED "THE GREAT COMMUNICATOR." HE HAD YEARS OF PRACTICE—HE ACTED IN MORE THAN 50 MOVIES!

REAGAN AND GORBACHEV WORKED TOGETHER TO BUILD A BETTER RELATIONSHIP BETWEEN THE UNITED STATES AND THE SOVIET UNION. EVENTUALLY, THE SOVIET UNION BROKE APART INTO MANY INDIVIDUAL COUNTRIES, INCLUDING RUSSIA.

THE FALL OF THE BERLIN WALL

THE BERLIN WALL WAS BUILT IN 1961 TO SEPARATE EAST GERMANY, WHICH WAS COMMUNIST, FROM WEST GERMANY, WHICH WASN'T. THE WALL STOOD FOR ALMOST 30 YEARS, UNTIL NOVEMBER 9, 1989. THAT DAY, TRAVEL WAS OPENED BETWEEN EAST AND WEST GERMANY. MANY EAST GERMANS CLIMBED ON TOP OF THE WALL TO CELEBRATE THEIR NEW FREEDOM TO TRAVEL TO WEST GERMANY. PEOPLE THEN BEGAN TEARING DOWN THE WALL WITH TOOLS—AND EVEN THEIR HANDS!

SEPTEMBER 11, 2001

September 11, 2001, was one of the most terrible days in US history. Almost 3,000 people were killed when **terrorists** crashed airplanes into the World Trade Center in New York City, the Pentagon in Washington, DC, and a field in Pennsylvania. That night, Americans turned to President George W. Bush for comfort as he addressed the country.

BEHIND THE WORDS

THE UNITED STATES AND ITS ALLIES ARE STILL FIGHTING TERRORISTS IN AN ONGOING CONFLICT CALLED THE WAR IN AFGHANISTAN.

Bush told the American people, "Terrorist attacks can shake the foundations of our biggest buildings, but they cannot touch the foundation of America." His words helped soothe a shocked and frightened nation by addressing Americans' fears and promising that the United States would bring the people responsible for the terrorist attacks to justice. Bush also reminded people of "the best of America"—the Americans who helped others that day.

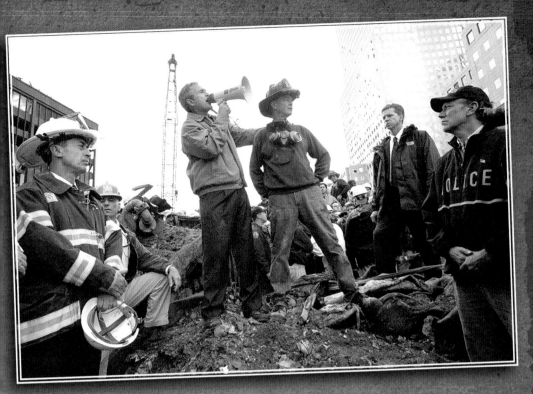

GEORGE W. BUSH REMINDED AMERICANS, "OUR COUNTRY IS STRONG." HE BELIEVED SOME OF THE BEST EXAMPLES OF THAT STRENGTH WERE THE MEN AND WOMEN HELPING AT GROUND ZERO.

"I CAN HEAR YOU"

BUSH VISITED THE SITE WHERE THE WORLD TRADE CENTER ONCE STOOD—THEN KNOWN AS GROUND ZERO—ON SEPTEMBER 14, 2001. WHILE HE WAS THERE, HE SPOKE TO FIRST RESPONDERS, SUCH AS FIREFIGHTERS, WORKING AT THE SITE. HE TOLD THEM, "I CAN HEAR YOU. THE REST OF THE WORLD HEARS YOU. AND THE PEOPLE WHO KNOCKED THESE BUILDINGS DOWN WILL HEAR ALL OF US SOON." THAT MESSAGE WAS RECORDED BY TV CAMERAS AND PLAYED AROUND THE WORLD.

"A SKINNY KID WITH A FUNNY NAME"

On November 4, 2008, Barack Obama was elected president of the United States. That night, he spoke in front of a crowd in Chicago, Illinois, to celebrate his victory. Although he hadn't taken the oath of office yet, the words Obama said that night showed the nation the direction of his presidency.

"This victory alone is not the change we seek. It is only the chance for us to make that change," Obama said. Obama himself was a symbol of change—the country's first African American president. However, he knew he'd have to work hard to have a lasting impact on important issues facing Americans. Obama fought for affordable health care for all, supported same-sex marriage, and inspired young people to stand up for what they believe.

BEHIND THE WORDS

BARACK OBAMA'S PRESIDENTIAL CAMPAIGN **SLOGAN** WAS "YES WE CAN." IN HIS FAREWELL ADDRESS IN 2017, HE TOLD AMERICANS TO REMAIN POSITIVE: "YES WE CAN. YES WE DID. YES WE CAN."

MAKING THE MOST OF A MOMENT

On July 27, 2004, Obama, who was running for US Senate, gave a speech at the Democratic National Convention. In this speech, which was shown on television and online, Obama talked about his childhood as "a skinny kid with a funny name" and his belief that "There's not a black America and white America and Latino America and Asian America; there's the United States of America." This speech is known as the moment that kicked off Obama's journey to the White House.

BARACK OBAMA'S WIFE, MICHELLE, BECAME A POPULAR FIRST LADY BECAUSE SHE IS A POWERFUL SPEAKER LIKE HE IS.

CONGRATULATIONS CHICAGO'S OWN

BARACK OBAMA

PRESIDENT-ELECT OF THE UNITED STATES OF AMERICA
-Mayor Richard M. Daley

YES WE CAN

CHANGES IN COMMUNICATION

From the earliest days of the United States, Americans have wanted to hear their leaders' ideas. At first, they had to hear the president speak in person or wait for the president's words to be printed in newspapers. Later, they could hear the president speak on the radio. Today, these options are still available, but people can also watch presidential speeches on television or online. Presidents use **social media** to communicate with people around the world, too.

BEHIND THE WORDS

IN 1949, HARRY TRUMAN WAS THE FIRST US PRESIDENT TO HAVE HIS INAUGURAL ADDRESS BE SHOWN ON TELEVISION. BILL CLINTON'S SECOND INAUGURATION SPEECH WAS THE FIRST TO BE STREAMED ONLINE, IN 1997.

Presidents' words remain extremely powerful, no matter how they're communicated. They have led to wars, created social change, and inspired people for hundreds of years. A president's words have real influence, and it's an essential part of the job to use that influence for the good of the country!

FAMOUS PRESIDENTIAL SPEECHES

1789: GEORGE WASHINGTON BECOMES THE FIRST US PRESIDENT TO TAKE THE OATH OF OFFICE.

1796: WASHINGTON DELIVERS HIS FAREWELL ADDRESS.

1823: JAMES MONROE OUTLINES THE MONROE DOCTRINE.

1863: ABRAHAM LINCOLN DELIVERS THE GETTYSBURG ADDRESS.

1933: FRANKLIN D. ROOSEVELT DELIVERS HIS FIRST INAUGURAL ADDRESS.

1941: ROOSEVELT ASKS CONGRESS TO DECLARE WAR ON JAPAN AFTER THE ATTACK ON PEARL HARBOR.

1962: KENNEDY DECLARES THAT THE UNITED STATES WILL GO TO THE MOON BEFORE THE END OF THE 1960s.

1965: LYNDON B. JOHNSON STATES "WE SHALL OVERCOME" IN HIS VOTING RIGHTS ADDRESS.

1974: RICHARD NIXON ANNOUNCES HIS PLAN TO RESIGN.

1987: RONALD REAGAN TELLS MIKHAIL GORBACHEV TO "TEAR DOWN THIS WALL!"

2001: GEORGE W. BUSH SPEAKS TO THE NATION AFTER THE SEPTEMBER 11 TERRORIST ATTACKS.

2008: BARACK OBAMA DELIVERS A VICTORY SPEECH AFTER BEING ELECTED THE FIRST BLACK PRESIDENT.

PRESIDENT TRUMP ON TWITTER

ALTHOUGH BARACK OBAMA WAS THE FIRST PRESIDENT TO USE THE SOCIAL MEDIA PLATFORM KNOWN AS TWITTER TO SEND SHORT MESSAGES, DONALD TRUMP BECAME THE MOST WELL-KNOWN PRESIDENTIAL "TWEETER." TRUMP HAS USED TWITTER TO TALK ABOUT HIS PLANS FOR THE COUNTRY, TO SHARE HIS THOUGHTS ON PROBLEMS IN THE WORLD, AND TO LET HIS FOLLOWERS KNOW WHAT HE THINKS OF OTHER LEADERS.

GLOSSARY

activism: using or supporting strong actions to help make changes in politics or society

assert: to say in a strong and definite way

bigotry: behaviors or beliefs associated with people who treat members of certain groups with hatred and intolerance

corollary: something that follows something or results from something else

dedication: an event to mark the official completion of something

doctrine: a statement of government policy, especially about international issues

infamy: being known for bad things or for evil

Latin American: having to do with the Americas south of the United States

scandal: an event in which people are shocked and upset because of acts that are morally or legally wrong

slogan: words that are easy to remember and grab attention

social media: websites and applications, or apps, that allow users to interact with each other and create online communities

Soviet Union: a former communist country that stretched from eastern Europe to Asia and was also known as the USSR

terrorist: one who uses violence and fear to challenge an authority

FOR MORE INFORMATION

BOOKS

Barber, James. *Presidents*. New York, NY:
DK Publishing, 2017.

Corey, Shana. *A Time to Act: John F. Kennedy's Big Speech*.
New York, NY: NorthSouth Books, 2017.

Sjonger, Rebecca. *Abraham Lincoln: The Gettysburg Address*. New York, NY: Crabtree Publishing Company, 2019.

WEBSITES

Famous Presidential Speeches
millercenter.org/the-presidency/presidential-speeches
Read, watch, or listen to speeches of every US president.

Our Documents
www.ourdocuments.gov/index.php
Learn the stories behind some of the most important words in US history, including the Gettysburg Address and Kennedy's inaugural address.

INDEX